POLAR BEARS

THE SEA MAMMAL DISCOVERY LIBRARY

Sarah Palmer

Rourke Enterprises, Inc.
Vero Beach, Florida 32964

Library of Congress Cataloging-in-Publication Data

Palmer, Sarah, 1955-
   Polar bears.

   (The Sea mammal discovery library)
   Includes index.
   Summary: Introduces the biggest, most
powerful Arctic animal—the white polar bear.
   1. Polar bear—Juvenile literature. [1. Polar bear]
I. Title.
II. Series: Palmer, Sarah, 1955-
Sea mammal discovery library.
QL737.C27P34   1989   599.74'446   88-26432
ISBN 0-86592-360-4

TABLE OF CONTENTS

POLAR BEARS

Polar bears are the biggest and most powerful animals in the Arctic **pack ice**. They fear no other animal. None are large enough to challenge the polar bear. Polar bears (*Thalarctos maritimus*) belong to the bear family. They are closely related to brown bears. Polar bears are as comfortable on land as in the water. They spend a lot of time on land and use the sea as a feeding ground.

Large, white polar bears have very powerful bodies

HOW THEY LOOK

Polar bears are covered in thick, creamy white fur. This fur keeps them warm and gives them good **camouflage** in the snowy landscape. An average male polar bear weighs over 1,000 pounds and is around ten feet long. Female polar bears are smaller, about eight feet long. Some Alaskan polar bears have weighed well over 1,500 pounds.

Well camouflaged in the snow, this polar bear lies down to rest

WHERE THEY LIVE

Polar bears are found only in the Arctic pack ice. When the ice melts in the summer, the bears move north. They return to the southern limits of the pack ice in the winter. Polar bear populations live in five countries: the United States, Canada, Greenland, the U.S.S.R., and Norway. The governments of all these countries have forbidden the hunting of polar bears.

Polar bears live in the cold Arctic pack ice

THEIR SENSES

Polar bears are curious animals. They often stand up on their hind legs to get a better look or sniff at things. They will follow the tracks of snow vehicles for miles. Like all animals, they have to rely on their senses to find food and fend off surprise attacks. Polar bears do not have very good eyesight. Luckily their sense of smell is excellent. Polar bears can smell a tasty seal from far away!

Polar bears stand on their hind legs
to have a good look around

Two polar bears play-fight on an Arctic summer's day

Polar bears sometimes drift for miles on ice floes

HUNTING PREY

Polar bears hunt alone. Their favorite food is seal meat, and they are especially fond of ringed seals. Polar bears **stalk** seals quietly and carefully. They crawl after them on their bellies, slipping in and out of the water between the **ice floes**. Polar bears have to attack on land because the seals are much too quick for them in the water. Polar bears only eat part of the seals. They leave the rest for Arctic foxes to eat.

Polar bears stalk their prey through water and over ice

WHAT THEY EAT

Polar bears are **carnivorous**, or meat-eating. In the summer months they sometimes eat leaves and berries, but they prefer meat. Polar bears eat about 8 pounds of meat each day. They eat all kinds of seals, fish, and other smaller sea **mammals**. Polar bears sometimes attack walrus herds. The walruses run to the sea for safety. Any that are left behind become easy **prey** for the polar bear.

Polar bears are at home both in and out of the water

LIVING IN THE OCEAN

Polar bears are very strong swimmers. They can keep up a steady speed of 6 M.P.H. over long distances. Polar bears use their front legs to propel themselves through the water. Their huge front paws make good paddles. The back legs are dragged behind to steer them. Polar bears can make shallow dives underwater and stay there for two minutes. They do not normally dive deeper than six feet.

Polar bears are strong swimmers

BABY POLAR BEARS

Polar bear **cubs** are born in the winter. A female polar bear normally has twin cubs every two or three years. The cubs are only 7 to 12 inches long when they are born, and they weigh under two pounds. Polar bear cubs are born in a **den** that their mother has dug under the snow. The female and her cubs stay together inside the den for about three months. The cubs feed on their mother's rich milk.

A female polar bear leads her cub to the ocean to hunt for food

THE POLAR BEAR FAMILY

The polar bears leave the den for the first time in the spring months of March or April. The cubs are now strong and healthy. They weigh about 20 pounds. The mother bear is hungry. She did not eat all the time she was in the den and is half her normal weight. Now the mother bear needs food, and she will teach her cubs to hunt. They love to play in the snow! A year later the cubs are big enough to look after themselves.

GLOSSARY

camouflage (KAM uh flazh) — a way of hiding by blending in with
   the surroundings

carnivorous (car NIV uh rus) — meat-eating

cub (CUB) — a baby polar bear

den (DEN) — a hole dug under the snow where baby polar bears
   are born

ice floe (ISE floe) — a large, floating chunk of ice

mammals (MAM uls) — animals that give birth to live young and
   feed them with mother's milk

pack ice (PAK ise) — an area where pieces of ice float close
   together in the sea

prey (PRAY) — an animal hunted by another for food

stalk (STAHK) — to follow quietly, ready to attack

INDEX